A RAY OF LIGHT

Reaches Down To Man

God is crying into the dark,
seeking mankind who is
in the darkness, crying.

JEWEL SPARKS

A RAY OF LIGHT
REACHES DOWN TO MAN

iUniverse books may be ordered through booksellers or by contacting:

iUniverse
1663 Liberty Drive
Bloomington, IN 47403
www.iuniverse.com
844-349-9409

ISBN: 978-1-5320-9347-0 (sc)
ISBN: 978-1-5320-9348-7 (hc)
ISBN: 978-1-5320-9346-3 (e)

Library of Congress Control Number: 2020916879

Print information available on the last page.

iUniverse rev. date: 09/22/2020

God is crying into the dark seeking mankind
who is in the dark, crying. - JS 2012.

As you face each day,
ask for God's impact
on all you say and do. He
Will do marvelous things
right before your eyes.
Ask for the courage to
Walk through each door He
opens.

May God Be Yours,
Jewel Sparks

WOULDN'T YOU RATHER

Is. 25:1 (NIV)

O Lord, You are my God; I will exalt you
and praise your name, for in perfect
faithfulness You have done marvelous things, planned long ago.

Hide me in Your hand
So no one can see
My brokenness You have planned.

Brokenness is not my choice
But I must let God lead
For I know He loves me most.

He holds me through the pain
Yet I don't want anyone to know
That this could be God's plan.

Often I fight God's design
Planned long ago
Please, put Your hand in mine.

My pride gets in the way
of what God is doing
Using me to speak what He has to say.

Unavailable, I hide in the dark
Thinking God can't find me,
He says "I will help you do your part".

I don't want this game
The acting out and medicine!
I don't feel like myself, not the same.

I would like to hide from myself.
What is God doing?
Maybe I'll put my faith on the shelf!

I haven't been talking to God much.
Confused, I choose to step away
Even though I believe in purpose, not luck.

Time passed and my faith stood still
Because of pills every day,
I was numbed, unable to feel.

Life moved in a slow pace
Foggy and sleepy
I lived in a daze.

One day, the light came on
God was on my side,
Forming me to get a job done.

Using my illness to heal others,
God took me inside hospitals
Presenting the gospel, doing what matters.

Embracing scripture, it dissolving my strife
The fog was lifting
My head was clearing, returning to life.

I was beginning to understand
The path God was forming
Touching the hurting, extending a hand.

After my 3rd hospital stay
And MUCH counseling
I began finding God's way.

I took my faith off the shelf
And I asked God
Would He, please, heal myself?

Bipolar Disorder isn't grand,
But it made me become
clay in the Father's hand.

With 3 stays, I could see God at work.
Using biblical truths
The staff gave me a puzzled look.

"How did she get answers we only know?"
God gave me simple replies
The power of God was beginning to show.

As I stay in the Potter's Hands,
Being formed by Him
I know I will find His peace in His plans.

If God asks you to be broken
To bring others to heaven,
Wouldn't you rather be sick?

~JS
2017

Although things are not perfect
Because of trial or pain, continue in thanksgiving
Even when the times are hard
Fierce winds are bound to blow
God is forever able
Start every day with worship
Yes, there'll be good times and yes some will be bad, but...
Zion waits in glory.. .where none are ever sad.

ABC'S OF HEALTH
AND HAPPINESS

A. Activity keeps life fresh and challenging.

B. Be yourself. You didn't just happen. You are a mosaic: many parts put in place with a purpose.

C. Communicate how you feel and express your needs. Few words go a long way.

D. Discipline is learned, but only if you get up after you stumble.

E. Examine all that comes your way. Grasp what brings truth and wholeness to body, mind, and spirit.

F. Forget the past; you cannot change it. To build a desirable future, start in the present.

G. Grow daily, don't ever stop going forward. Success will come if you invest in the journey.

H. Harmony is a song the heart sings because even good comes from the rain clouds.

I. Individualism is your greatest asset. A rainbow's beauty comes from its many colors.

J. Joy comes from obedience and sacrifices of the heart.

K. Kindness can never be overdone. It gives birth to compassion.

L. Laugh at yourself and with others often.

M. Many roads lead you astray. Pick the one you will be glad you traveled.

N. Not every teacher allows you the freedom to learn...and fail.

O. Opportunity knocking? Open the door.

P. Possessions-it is not what you have-it is what you do with what you have.

Q. Quit the negative! Enjoy life and celebrate the small things.

R. Right living helps you make healthy choices and the ability to follow them.

S. Self: Take care of yourself. No one else will find the answers you prefer.

T. Truthfulness keeps you from having to pay the price of lying.

U. Understanding and being understood requires you to stop and listen.

V. Very important things are often overlooked. Don't be hasty, stop-consider-choose.

W. Weather clouds are always changing. Life passes in seasons.

X. Examine your heart-harbor the good things and let the rest drift away.

Y. Yearn for the good, the lovely, and the fun.

Z. Zest of life comes from listening to your heart, your neighbor and your God

-JC May-2012

ALONE WITH RAGE

The pain runs deep
Tears run down my cheek
My words considered void
My ideas, they quickly avoid
From those I hope to hold dear
My words are cloudy and unclear
They are confused by my anger
I feel as if they don't care
I hate the rage boiling within me
It is the pain yet they cannot see
I only want to share all I live and learn
To show what causes my passions to burn
But most often what I offer is cast aside
My heart is broken, my esteem is cold inside
Only because I try to share
With those I thought would care

J. C. 2013

A LOVING WORK

In my frustration, I forgot to talk to You.
Life was distorted; I couldn't see what was true.
Darkness loomed and my anger grew.

It wasn't black and white but red not within,
I knew I was in trouble. Anger was eating at me
God, by Your grace, set me free.

On my knees, asking God to take me in,
Please hold me close and let healing begin.
You, alone, can melt my heart of sin.

I feel Your presence upon me,
The hardness inside me is fading.
Thanks for Your loving work in me.

~JS
2017

AS YOU DESIRE

Hot tears running down my face
My anger burned, boiling mad
I must allow myself some space
Taking a deep breath, Lord, bring peace.

Having hurt, I broke someone's heart
Crying in the dark, overwhelmed
It was my fault. I had let it start,
Finding a way to humbly apologize.

Bitterness faded, agony disappears
Speech returned with repentant words.
My heart softened, the Lord touched my tears,
Deep inside, joy began to grow.

May I guard my anger, making it count,
Always to do a work, with a purpose,
Not wasting the energy making the tears flow out.
Lord, help me to live life as you desire.
JC ~ 2016

AGAIN AT 55 MY HEART SINGS

To fall in love at 55
My heart aches to be alive
To have a second love
The perfect man from above
This, the song of my heart
To be with him, Lord, give me a start
May I share my life with him?
Loneliness leaves, joy begins!
Together our lives belong.
Because God Himself, sings the song!

J. C. 4-20-2013

AT HIS FEET

Let's ask God to stretch out his hand
Reaching down to help us take a stand
Against that which He calls wrong
Because sin kills what makes us strong.
God's way always has a price
To pay, accompanied by a sacrifice
The cost may hurt but it makes us grow
Holding on to Jesus, His light begins to show
All around us, many choices to make
Big God and little gods who do we take?
Made it be JHWH God, His love so sweet
We embrace with our lives placed at his feet.
2013

BITING BAIT

Matthew 4:19 (AMP) "And I will make <u>you Fishers of Men</u>."

When the Apostle Peter, went fishing, I wonder if he ever thought of this: "if you give a man a fish – you feed him for a day – teach a man to fish and you feed him for a lifetime!"

Have you ever been fishing? I went a few times as a child. I watched my dad packing his tackle box a certain way to lure the fish he wanted for dinner that night! FYI: You must bait your hook with whatever the fish want for dinner!

We must learn the best bait to use where ever we go to feed others.

-Fish will only bite when hungry.
-What bait makes you hungry?

When we fish, we rarely get it right on the first bite like the fish do. Yes, maybe the fish can. It could be his first bite and his first time on dad's dinner plate!

What are you feeding on? Did you find the fish with the gold coin in his mouth?

JS
2017

CLUTCH ME CLOSE

Everyone faces sin
No matter what shape you're in
Sin grabs at you for control
To master your life, wherever you go

The unsaved hang with the devil, swapping ideas
Hearts harden, giving evil, their wills
The handcuffs of darkness create,
Building bondages-addictions they make

Those who allow evil to dwell in their hearts
Hold on to destruction, giving it power to start
The handcuffs of darkness, grasping tightly
Holding you captive, thinking nobody can see

The price you pay to make hurtful choices your way
It will always cost more than you can ever pay
Stealing the ones you love and need so much
Ask God to pull you close, free from the devil's clutch.

~JS
2017

COFFEE! COFFEE! COFFEE!

Are you really my friend?
Starting at age 12, is this the end?
Doctor said "Only drink decaf!"
"Cut your caffeine more than in half."

The gift you receive will be sweet
A sound night of wonderful sleep!
So, take the challenge of going without
What you call a friend, yet you doubt.

Friends don't steal important things
But help you find what makes you sing.
Coffee will remind me of Melissa's love;
Helping me do the hard thing from above.

Making me watch my sleep
Which a 'no coffee promise,' I don't want to keep.
But, her strength in helping me says "No"
Bringing health between a mother and daughter grow.

~JS
July 27, 2019 - Thursday

COMING YOUR WAY

This little box is coming your way

"I love you" is what it means to say!

If I had my wish, on this day,

It would be me coming to play

I will see you soon, I tell myself everyday

To hug and kiss you! If I had my way

So I put on a smile and save my pay

Knowing I will see you soon, I pray.

4-12-14

THE DANCE

My hurt is so deep
Because he chose his sin to keep
He says I am outside what he nurtures
A fantasy of addicting pictures.

I can't seem to let go of him
At least twelve years it has been
I have guarded my heart
Hoping to join in a Godly start.

I pray to see God's loving hand
Touch the heart of him who was my man
Help him see his choices bring destruction
They drive him to unhealthy obsessions.

Does it really enrich his life?
Does he have a real or fake "wife"?
God heal this dance in the mind
By purging the heart of mankind.

-JS
2018

DEEP PAIN

How do I pray when hurt is so deep? A pain so strong it appears every day
Trying so hard to push it aside
It doesn't listen to me even when I pray

I've been told it isn't my fault Standing before God, I find innocence
Yet I know His love will carry me
Through this painful internal occurrence

Knowing God sees how I suffer, Seeing Jesus on the cross, He felt it too
With His great wisdom I look to see
Hoping His Word will guide me through

This anger I hold has a grip I can't let go reoccurring a long, long time
Just can't shake it loose
Throwing things, I wish it wasn't mine

Maybe if I break my things on the outside the power of the flesh I won't obey
Perhaps, I can hear God's still small voice
Tell me how to stop the pain, making the hurt go away.
~JS
2017

Exodus 32:19

As Moses lays on his face worshipping the
Invisible God from the top of Mt. Sinai, his
Brother was at the foot of Mt. Sinai fashioning
Visible, calf-like God from gold for people
Whose hearts were made of stone.
Paraphased

7-18-14

EMBRACE

I find myself struggling to live with you.
Your actions or maybe your words make me blue.
Will it always hurt no matter what I do?

I pray to God to unravel this mess.
Asking in prayer, each day I access.
What to do, that the pain would be less.

I know God's hand in mine
Helping me get through tough times,
Taking one step, beholding God is divine.

To live with others
Will always be a bother.
I need to talk to the Father.

While kneeling in His presence,
I find my negative occurrence.
Fading, I give all an embrace!

~JC
2016

EXCUSES! EXCUSES! EXCUSES!

"Today, if you hear His voice,
Do not harden your hearts" Heb. 3:7,8 NIV

Look for excuses to shine your light for Jesus. Find
a chance to give a hug, a smile or even a Bible
verse. In the name of Jesus, reach out and bring
encouragement. Use your excuses to change
lives, to become more like Jesus and to walk in victory!

As we lay down our lives, let's pick up more
Excuses to serve Him.

God, give us excuses to better serve you. By your power, with
Your design, help us use our opportunities wisely. Amen

Is Opportunity Knocking?

EYES WIDE SHUT

Ever since the world began
No one has been able to open
The eyes of someone born blind:
If this man were not from God,
He could not have done it.
John 9:32, 33 NLT

The son physically could not see.
His parents spiritually could not see.
The paradox of life,
When the blind can see
While their eyes are still shut
And others stumble in the dark
With their eyes wide open.

FATHER'S DAY 2005

Today I would like to make a little fuss over you
Although you were never one who would require it
It comes from my heart, expressing my love
I know you wouldn't ask for it, you'd just desire it.

Growing up, love was always expressed
With hugs and kisses openly displayed
"I love you's spoken to each other
Kind words given generously every day.

So with much affection and love
A token gift I give to you
To let you know I cherish this love
You've given me my whole life through.

JS
2005

THE FLOWER

I give myself permission to walk a negative path
It is obstructive, raising God's wrath
There is no benefit or constructive thing.
It mimics darkness. My heart can't sing
I seek the Lord in prayer, down on my knees
That He alone my heartache can ease
Letting go of all my rights, my flesh dies
A small seed within my heart begins to rise.
Its beauty surpasses all ugliness
A delicate and gentle flower it is
Changing my heart, becoming more like His.

-JC
2014

FRIENDS

Friends are people we let inside
To see what we struggle to hide
Even with Jesus, we fail to abide,
Following God, where ever He would guide.

Friends bring you before the Lord
Breaking the hard stuff with His two-edged sword
By phone or text, you can share what you heard,
Embracing your favorite, of God's Holy Word.

If at your new place, you become kinda blue
Go to the bathroom mirror and this is what to do
Your teeth are like your friends no matter where you move
Those pearly whites
Will be smiling right back at you!

~JC
2015

FROM MY HEART

Seeking your presence
Where I find quiet stillness,
Where I draw close to You
I find calmness like no other.

When I seek Your presence
My heart is made new
I am able to let go choosing to walk with You.
I see the vain fall off and embrace what is true –You

All that hinders me – the anger or criticism
I am willing to lay down for You to change me
You show true values, worth living for
To esteem my brother's worth, this I begin to see.

To love those who cause me pain
Your touch renews my heart again
I walk away feeling better than before
For You cause my heart to sing.

As this Labor of Love comes to an end,
You will find God's next endeavor right around the corner.

With fresh eyes, God will show you His path of wholeness and
holiness.
It won't be easy, but it will be worth every step.

God's call may cost more than we expected, yet, to be in His presence is priceless.
Even with our mistakes, God will re-mold them, using them for good.

With joyful obedience, He makes our hearts sing, equipping us even on our darkest days.
Being diligent to do all He might ask.

I am given healing from the past, joy throughout today, and guidance to face tomorrow.
Hand in hand, I am so glad I need Him.

JC 2014

-Adapted from several sources

GROANING

Looking down at the world He made
The Father groans
As Eve picks fruit in the shade
The Father groans

With deep heartache from sin's cost
Jesus groans
For mankind, He bears the cross
Jesus groans

Speaking words man cannot find
The Spirit groans
In intercession, He heals mankind
The Spirit groans

Futile searches to find purpose
We groan
Knowing all our efforts are pointless.
We groan

With a hand of mercy, God reaches down
He groans
The day has come, He must strike His Son
He groans

God knows someday His Beloved will come
God groans
The trumpet calls the Bride to come
God groans, with joy
~JC~ *2014*

HARD AS BRASS

When the heavens are hard as brass,
When your banquet tastes like grass,
When life is empty and cold,
When, your heart's desire turns to mold.

There is no joy under heaven for you
There is no acknowledgement to do
There the ground is so hard the rain can't refresh
There hearts of gods whose purpose banish.

Look toe God who breaks the brass heavens
Look in the face of God who loves us.
Look at the vanity you have in your hands
Look at your shackles drop to the ground.

He dissolves our sins
He waters our souls
He fills our hearts with joys.
He brings all our needs.

Jesus, the one who gives,
Renews,
Provides,
His love is best of all!
~JC 2015

"Though the mountains be shaken and the hills be removed, yet my unfailing love for you will not be shaken nor my covenant of peace be removed." Is 54:10 (NIV)

HAZY, CRAZY LIFE

When life is crazy
God's voice seems hazy.
Maybe there's a new plan
That you don't understand.

God's the potter, we are the clay.
He chooses to make us His way.
A divine path; God will make
the only way worth to take.

The price might be hard to pay,
But, it is really the best way!
Hand in hand, God will guide.
He will never leave your side!

~JC
2013

HEARING TO GROW

Romans 10:17
Faith comes by hearing, not by seeing.
How often we get these two mixed up
We think our faith will grow by
seeing the miracles of God. But it
Is really by hearing the promises of God

Is not that I need more miracles to see,
but, to hear God's voice when He speaks to me.

This is the avenue God has chosen
to make faith grow within my bosom.

THE HURT

J. C. 5-31-2013

If I hurt I should find someone who cares
To discuss my heartache and fears
It seems the more I share what I see
That which I'm carrying deep inside of me

My A to speak about what causing my heartache!
Here we go with round 2-I'm the angry crazy one
I thought reaching out would get the job done

But I find harsh words again are aimed at me
I wasn't looking for excuses but a remedy.
I came to talk this situation through
So busy to tell me what to do, I walk away with injury number 2.

I came to you because I thought you could
Help me sort this out and feel how I should
My feeling ignored while your advice was expressed that day
I felt so hurt so I walked away

IMPORTANT

Dear Lord, I know You love me everyday
but why do you shape my life this way?
Would a man cause me to love You less?
I really do want to love You best.

Is Your plan for me to love only one man?
I look around to find him if I can.
But, he never comes seeking to find me
Lord, help me desire to serve You on bended knee.

Yielding my heart for You to fill
Keep my life pure by doing Your will
In Your hands, remaining still
Help me stay on the Potter's Wheel.

I know I am human; You are divine
I presume to know Your design
What 1 thought You chose, never comes to be
Make whatever is important to You, important to me.
~JS
2018

IMMEASURABLE

Ephesians 3:20,21 (NIV)

20: ow to him who is able to do immeasurably more than all we ask or imagine, according to his power that is at work within us, 21: to him be glory in the church and in Christ Jesus throughout all generations, for ever and ever! Amen.

That which is Immeasurable:

–The sand on the beach

–The snow on the mountains

–The stars in the sky

–The drops in the ocean

–The joy of a newborn baby

–The depth of God's forgiveness

–The power in God's promises that never fail

Most of all His matchless love!

J.S. 2014
11-14-14

IMPOSSIBILITY

Grow feathers
Breathe sand
Quench thrist with crackers
Make a meal of ketchup

Out Give God's Grace
By His grace, He
Gives us His love and
Grace every time
We seek Him - every
Need, every moment
and every endeavor.

It is impossible for God to
Ignore us when we cry out
for His help because He loves us.

-JS
2017

IN THE BOTTLE

The little boy hugged his mother's leg
A tear rolled down his dirty cheek.
Every day his tummy would ache,
Needing food and water, hunger cries

A slap across the face, again, tonight
Black and blue, a bruise shows itself
Day after day, she bares the fight
Where to find the love she's hungry for.

He knows his pain carries a purpose,
The Hand of God gives him strength.
So he doesn't have to live with less
God sees every tear, He knows we cry.

Into a bottle Our Lord puts our tears
He wants to show us He knows every pain.
Someday, God will turn the tears into cheers
Our pain will cease into joy evermore.

INTO MY WORLD

Home is not where you hang your hat
or discard your shoes on the front mat.
But it is here you lay,
the troubles you've gathered along the way.
Receiving strength from above
we find faith, hope, and love.

To be like Jesus, my highest call
I labor each day, lest I fall.
My heart is so dirty, my tongue is black
A temper so hot, patience I lack.
But God in His grace, extends a hand
making me strong; so I can stand

I found God's presence restoring my life,
doing the impossible, removing the strife.
I was changing, love and peace came to dwell,
I knew God was real; His love had made me well.

J. C. 2012

I must walk in obedience and die to the flesh!

Do not believe the lie of the devil!

JS
2017

JOY IN LIVING

If I could choose my way to live
Things would look different.
Sharing encouraging words to give
Living abundantly, feasting on the Word.

This is a great idea, doing it everyday
Those rain clouds shrink and disappear
And things begin to go a healthy way
Sunshine slowly warms your heart.

I know we think negativity is our right
People hurt us so we are sassy back
I ask myself: Is all this distress worth it?
Clinging to this hurt just makes life a mess!

Please Lord; help me walk by Your side
To let go of that which pushes You away
Renew brotherly love. Make it grow inside.
Changing me to reflect Your love and joy.
JS
2017

JOY, LAUGHTER, AND GLEE

The stars shine brightly
The roses smell sweetly
The birds chirp a morning song
God, how did you make me?

My kids have grown to maturity
In many ways they care for me
They understand what I don't get
Electronics, and all technology.

In many ways the tables have turned
The kids have become smarter than me
My job is to love them and learn from them
Their lives bring me joy, laughter, and glee.

~JS
2019

KIDDING IN PRINEVILLE

Peyton and Austin in the kitchen, cooking blueberry pancakes and eggs a
flipping. My grandsons; I stand there looking.

Time has been good, they have grown so big. Serious one moment the next,
dancing a jig. So glad not to miss this! I really am digging it.

Melissa, staining wood, built by Josh. He sees her handiwork –
"Oh My Gosh!"
Is he looking at his wife or the job done with a brush?

Never a dull moment around here; jokes told even when no smiles appear.
When I find a place in Prineville I will cheer

~JS
2019

KNOCK! KNOCK!

Sin fights everybody
Everybody fights sin

Sin influences everybody
Everybody is influenced by sin

Sin battles us everyday
Everybody battles sin everyday

Pick your battles and your armor
Choosing the right armor brings success

But we must let God fight for us
His power fights while we watch His might

Sin always destroys all it touches
Sin always will be destroyed by God's touch

Sin requires you to do nothing
Sin in God's Hands becomes nothing

So the next time the devil comes knocking,
Ask Jesus to answer the door!
~JS
2019

THE LIGHT

We love because He first loved us. John 4:19 (NIV)

1. We did not receive God's love on our own
2. Thinking my actions would make love grow
3. Doing good deeds, saying kind words
4. Would cause those blue feelings to go
5. Even on a good day we hang onto self
6. Putting their needs back on the shelf.

The hurts center only on our concerns
Looking for relief, we focus just on my years.
Helpless and hopeless, there is no way,
To turn things around, and make a better day.

After much struggle, I just want to quit
Because, even with tears and anger, I just don't get it.
I want to walk in peace and joy
With a smile and kindness, this is what I would enjoy.
But nothing makes me happy, not even a toy

God, work on my insides where love begins
Because I know it is not what I hold in my hands
But to sit in Your arms, You holding me tight
Removing my sin and turning on Your light.

LISTENING

Wrapped in warm blankets, the alarm sounds.
It can't be morning yet. I turn over
Trying t grab a little more shut eye
Just a little more sleep and I'll feel better

Oh, the buzzer! Does the clock lie?
I had better get up, lots to do today
The laundry...what's for dinner?
Crock Pot! Nice and easy I say.

Jesus, how did you do all the Bible says?
Disciples fussing back and forth
Healing the sick, feeding thousands
And loving them like never before!

Jesus slips away, be it dawn or dusk
Approaching the Father for rest and power
He knew the path ahead would use His pain for job
Equipped by God's hand, He could face that dark hour.

When you are carrying a heavy load
Find a quiet place and slip away
Where you can stop and look to Jesus
And listen to what He has to say.

1-15

MORE OF JESUS

Who do I think I am?
Every day I tell God what to do!
My ideas must be the best for me.
Like God needs my input a time or two!

"It makes God laugh when we tell Him our plans"
As if we know what we need the most
Commanding God to give me every desire
I follow the path of my choosing, and I become lost.

Still I tell God, "Give me a Christian Man!"
Is totally wrong! Speak what God finds true
God would pick someone different for me
One who lives and loves God more than I do.

~ JS
2018

MOVING MOTIVATES ME

Reaching goals I have set motivates me but, set too low, a challenge doesn't exist, you see
Set too high, it becomes quite overwhelming. Goals will help push me forward so I can succeed.

Motivation means finding what makes me go! Digging and learning skills I didn't know.
Step by step, day by day, progress will show amazing things that will help me to grow!

Check your self-talk, what do you say? Does it tear you down or help along the way?
Positive thoughts bring sunshine into your day, chasing dark and dreary clouds away!

Learning and climbing, your healing will grow, finding strength within, you didn't know.
Deep within a Divine touch begins to show. God gives wisdom for today and tomorrow.

So, keep going, facing the goals you have set. It gets harder the farther along you get
Hang in there. Don't allow yourself to quit. You will love the new you your hard work has begat.

Just dangle that carrot, whatever it takes to keep moving forward at your own pace.
Find what you need to finish the race but, the best prize will be the smile on your face!

~JC~ 7/8/14

MY STRETCHER

When life stretches,
I call you, Lord, cuz I know you see!
Your love and provisions care for me.

I suppose I could find my way,
But life's path will often decay.
I need to hear you tell me what to say.

The world offers crutches or a walker.
You get meds and advice from the doctor.
Although these work, remember, God is the author.

I picked up the walker, the doctor calls
He said, "This would help break my falls!"
It was like learning a new language after all.

As I struggle to live with this new skill,
I am glad it isn't another pill.
Your hand is my stretcher helping me to do Your will

NEVER ADULTS

As we stumble every day
Trying hard just to obey
Grace will be given to us to
Help us to walk in righteousness.
Going forward each step we take
In our youth a mistake we make
God looks down on His children below
Seeing, we simply need to grow
His adults, we will never become
But stay as a child in need of Him

J. C. 2012

ONE LINER'S

True faith never leaves a person unchanged.

Nothing changes without a burden.

We all have a mission field because our mess has given us a message.

He paid the price so I could receive the prize.

Will power won't work! My will power has won't power! - Doug Snow 2010

Never have to worry about a lifestyle of sin if you have a lifestyle of repentance.

~JS
2013

II Thess. 2: 11, 12

THE PERIL OF SILENCE

7-31-15

Why did you lay aside God's book?
To give sin a second look?
Walking in darkness, ahead, is a pit,
Easily you fall in it.

I'm stuck: "Help! I can't get out!
What is this torture all about?
I better not holler, someone might know,
that I'm here where I shouldn't go.

It is not that I can't get out
It's that I don't want to get caught
Compartmentalize is the game
To play I must hide my shame.

~JS
2015

PROSPECTIVE

Who will take care of me
When I can't get what I need?

The things I can do today
Might not always be that way.

Somethings I require to be just so,
Other things, I demand they must go!

It is not the only way I know
But I have a life of purpose and to grow.

Lord, I understand, your love is always grand.
I can tell You are there by the footprints in the sand.

Miracles do happen sometimes I know,
But I need to let my desires go.

Living for today is a better choice,
Following Jesus, who gives purpose.

Those hard times cause me to be stronger,
The joy God gives makes me laugh longer.

Putting a smile on my face each day,
Making those rain clouds go away.

Sometimes life is not what I see,
I must ask God to help me.

Often, I find myself focusing on temporal things.
But to live for Jesus, is what makes my heart sing.

Life can fool you, just look at the neighbor's lawn,
Time for an afternoon nap; he gives a yawn.

"Hey neighbor, your grass is so nice. How long did it take"?
With a wide grin, he said "Don't worry, it's fake!

~JC
2016

RADICAL ACCEPTANCE

Here is what I offered Kaiser Group on Radical Acceptance

For my homework I looked into Radical Acceptance on line. I found many video's, quotes, and books. Nearly every item was ear marked by Tara Brach. This concerned me because it appeared she had a corner of the market. Monopolies always raise a red flag.

Radical Acceptance comes from Buddhism. When I'm looking to learn, I always check out the author. Buddha never claimed deity, he said he wasn't the way but would show you the way.

Buddha is dead. His statues have eyes that cannot see and ears of stone which cannot hear. I don't understand how he can bring life and peace to mankind when he cannot think or even breathe.

I do find radical acceptance in my life when the Creator of all things radically reaches down and touches my life and I accept it.

11-24-14

REDEEMED

I was controlled by:
    Carnality
    Pointless Pain
    Wasted Wandering
    Sorrowful Sin
    Hollow Hope

I saw:
    Lasting Love
    Powerful Promises
    Constant Companionship
    Selfless Sacrifice
    Gracious Giving

I received:
    Teachable Truths
    Forgiving Faith
    Christ's Compassion
    Everlasting Eternity

~JS
2017

ROSES

The sweet smell of the Rose calls you
This flower is so beautiful too.
Look closely before you pick
Under the petals, the thorns will stick.

Under the pretty petals, the devil hides his tricks
Telling us Roses have no thorns that prick.
They come in most any hue
and, are given to say "I love you!"

Proceed with caution. The devil hides behind the lovely
He sets a snare for God's elect daily
While the devil is his mischief making,
The child of God is on his knees his Father seeking.

~JS
2019

June 14, 2013

Philippians 3:13-14 (NIV)

14: I press on toward the Goal to win the prize for
Which God has called me heavenward in Christ Jesus

13: But, one thing I do: Forgetting what is behind and straining
Toward what is ahead

RUN TO WIN

Embrace the desire
Establish the path
Carve out the plan
Sacrifice those obstacles
Train to become strong
Reach with a purpose
Press toward the prize
Stretch for the goal
Receive the crown
Giving God the glory

-JC 2013

RUSTY

I just wanted to quit
You are just the cause of it!
You hurt my feeling by what you say
It happens almost every day.

Yeah, I get in the flesh, my anger flares
Know what? I really don't care
You assume your answers are right
You're walking in the dark but you could be in the light.

I'll make my own choices up ahead
Speaking my words using ones from my head
God will probably tell me to repent
I know I'm in trouble for the words I sent.

Yeah, I'm on the other side of the fence
Doing and saying what doesn't make sense
I know obedience to God is best
But my heart is as stone and forgiveness is rust.
JS
2018

9/21/2013

Six days you shall labor and do all your work, but the seventh
day is the Sabbath of the Lord your God. In it you shall do no
work. Exodus 20:9-10

Slow down to see God working
Abide in God's presence
Biblical meditation practiced
Brotherly friendships strengthened
Acknowledge God's desires
Teaching from the Word
Heavenly Father seen anew

Marvel at God's handiwork Genesis 2:2
Receive God's deliverance Deuteronomy 5:12-15
Post God's ways and study them Deuteronomy 6:4-6
Honor God's covenants Exodus 31:12-18

Adapted from Our Daily Bread

SHAPED BY CHOICES

6-4-13

1. I give away personal peace
2. My priorities are turned upside down
3. I deny my faith to serve my own desires
4. I embrace stupidity
5. I kill my own joy
6. I push away from those who care
7. The choices I make are warped
8. I lay aside what is important
9. I'm willing to pay a high price to have my own foolishness
10. I lose sight of the truth
11. My silence hurts the innocent
12. I become part of the problem
13. I become unable to find Godly solutions
14. I belittle others
15. I waste time because life is precious
16. My life becomes unproductive
17. I embrace pointlessness because time, money, and energy lose value
18. My focus shifts away from eternal values
19. I become busy building regrets
20. My thoughts and actions damage the present
21. Negativity rules my thoughts and actions
22. Like a poison, negativity corrodes every aspect of my life
23. I do and say what I don't like, and what I desire I hadn't done

24. I destroy people and things I cherish
25. I cannot find a way out of my dilemma
26. I lay aside what is most important and the ability to go where I want.
27. I hurt myself
28. My life becomes unfruitful in God's hands
29. I regret what I have done and don't know if I can change the harm.
30. I become consumed by what I don't want to be
31. I must find better choices
32. I must ask God to show me how to let go of the pointless
33. Ask God for wisdom of healthy thoughts which develop Godly actions and attitudes.

SHOUTS SOFTLY SPOKEN

To be losing you yet you're
standing right in front of me.
You care as long as you don't
have to feel.

How do I stop the pain?

How do I go forward while
the pain keeps me frozen
in my tracks? I live between
numbness and rage. Inside me
is a battle between emotional
Destruction and a faith believing
God will never leave me to fight
alone.

I know the words that are
Spoken last are the most
remembered no matter how
Softly expressed.
God Help Me

~JC~
2016

SMILIN'

I just wanted to say "thanks" to you
The little book and candy so sweet;
The gifts and prayers you gave
Bless me so much! tis so neat!

Ever have "one of those" days?
Wondering how to make it through?
Then I remember God, Himself,
Is listening to prayers from you!

God promises if we ask. He will answer
Even when others approach Him for us
Your prayer puts a song in my heart
And His grace puts a smile on my face.

2-9-14

SIN

Sin will cost more than
You ever intended to pay

Sin will take you farther
Than you ever intended to go

Sin never tells the whole story
Sin is deceitful

Sin will keep you longer,
than you ever intended to stay.

-JC

SPROUTING

I need help which I can't ask for,
I build a wall of anger I hope you break through.

I hurt, I forget how it began
I wish not to be left alone.

In silent hostility I sit
Hoping your prayers would redirect it
Communication must come from outside of me

I am all locked up, can't find the key.
I don't like being this way
I know it doesn't bring happiness to your day
Like being in a pit, I need a hand to get out.

But, I can't speak or even give a shout.
A hug or a prayer seems to break my prison

The beginning of hope and compassion
Knowing I'm not alone I let go of my doubt
The wall cracks as joyful flowers sprout

JC

SOMEDAY

Why do I get offended?
Why do my feelings get hurt and I feel ignored?
I don't like flying solo
Sitting in silence, I'm never heard.

I busy myself alone in my room
Reading my Bible and making crafts too.
Maybe too much TV with negativity
I must have a nap or two.

Lord, why must I remain by myself?
Why are You painting my life so?
Someday I hope to find a brand new me,
Where I began praising you, letting my grumbling go!

SO SAD

Lord, why is this so bad?
It breaks my heart and makes me sad.
My pain I tried to share
I felt like they didn't care
Why did they get defensive, never seeing me?
I only came because I hurt which you couldn't see

So busy telling me how to change
My thoughts and words, I should rearrange
The next time I hurt, you can be glad
I won't come to you and make you sad.

6-1-2013

STOPPING

Hidden, yet Jesus and me,
Praying where no one can see
All interruptions left outside
In His presence I abide

I climb into my Father's arms
Here I find peace and no alarms
He helps me stop and pray
Before I begin my day

JC ~ 2015

THE SWEET AFTERMATH
OF SORROW

The sweetness of no coffee is deep sleep
To empower my days with new energy so sweet
Passing on caffeine will enable me to live
With joy, and productivity to give
Because my sleep will be sound
All the way around!
I will benefit

Friday, July 26, 2019

SWEET SACRIFICES

When the path of life is painfully dark
And every goal misses the mark.
Black clouds hover over head
Your life story doesn't read how you like it read.

How to change that which causes pain
Into that which brings life again
To see them grow in a way unexpected
Bring joy and life reflected.

To hear the kids giggle with mirth
Lightens the dark days healing my hurt
The price we pay for happiness and health
Is well worth sacrifices

JC
2014

Spiritual Food

We headed to our favorite restaurant for breakfast. This was our usual practice after Sunday service. I always wondered which I enjoyed the most - the fellowship or food. After a leisurely meal, we packed up our leftovers and headed for the door. Most everyone else left a dollar or two as a tip but I had developed a plan to always leave a Gospel of John booklet. We threaded our way through the hungry ones waiting. Opening the car door, I heard a man coming from the restaurant calling"Hey!, Hey! It was our waiter. "You forgot your book!" I gave a loud shout "No, that is for you!"

- JC
2014

Simply sincere
Up raised hands
Remolding to be done
Revealed by God
Effecting eternity
New understanding in Christ
Down from glory
Entering the heart of mankind
Rejoicing over
Everyone who would
Die to self so they could be.
    SURRENDERED!
        Into the hands of God.

-JS
2018
WM Retreat

THE SNOW'S I KNOW

I have a friend, Pastor Doug Snow.
His job is to equip us, helping us to grow
So, we can be like Jesus wherever we go.
If we need a hand or hug, I say, "Go to Snow"

Standing by him is Janet, the love of his life
Simply serving King Jesus, a virtuous wife
I find such joy in her laugh and her song
Smiling through my trials, she makes me strong.

Together they make the best team I know
Helping others to learn though it may be slow
But there is one thing I surely know
The Son shines at the church were the Snow's go

THAT SECOND LOOK!

To show God's hand,
I'd like for you to see
His power and love
Giving to you and me!

To gaze on earth, the sky above
both reflections of His love.
Reaching down, to help us find our way
God's mighty hand dissolves our fray.

Bringing purpose to the vanity of our days
I respond with heartfelt praise.
God alone brings reason to my mess
granting peace, joy, and tenderness.
Within His boundaries, I seek to be
for He alone knows what's good for me!
I hope you stop and take that second look
Because then you'll find God's face in His Book.

THIS IS THE HOUSE WHERE AUSTIN AND PEYTON LIVE

This is the house where Austin and Peyton live, with 2 crazy cats scratchin' to get in. Two little busy boys with a mischievous grin; they love their sweet momma from her head to her toes, making never-ending "projects" where ever she goes.

Her laundry's piled high, her favorite task, but that doesn't matter, she's quite the lass! Counting in the laundry room, hiding in the tub, is their favorite game, the one which they love!

With giggles and shouts, days pass one by one, hearts filled with joy, we are the blessed ones. Even though things get crazy and wild, the love we see is from the heart of a child. So when they want a bath and you want them in bed, pause for a moment, your hands holding your head. Look at the chaos you cannot overcome.

Remind yourself: It's like the beat of a drum; no music's complete without it. The rhythm clear and strong, what today makes your head hurt, someday will be a love song.

All things worth having must be practiced to grow; today you plant a seed, tomorrow it will show. The path you pave today, with your blood and tears, will cause those sprouts to be strong beyond their years.

When you are at the house of Austin and Peyton, plan to laugh a lot! And, the food is really great. You will find cars and Legos always under your feet, but it doesn't matter because Austin and Peyton are so very sweet!
2011

Thoughts of you
Hopeful truth
Incredible joy
Nice wonders
Kind actions
Immediate benefits
New beginnings
Grand events

Outstanding happenings
Fabulous days

Youthful energy
Outrageous friendships
Unbelievable living

Jewel 6-28-04

THINKING

3/27/2014

They said he's coming
I think
They changed the departure date
I think
The truth should settle down
I think
I'm more confused than they are
I think
The tickets are bought. He's coming
I think
His voice enters my dreams
I think
Three weeks, he plans to stay
I think
The job looks bigger than thought
I think
The task overwhelms me
I think
The Lord wants me to help
I think
Even though my flesh opposes
I think
With God's song with me
I go

THOSE SNOWS

"Come now, let us settle the matter,"
says the Lord.
"Though your sins are like scarlet,
they shall be as white as snow;
though they are red as crimson,
they shall be like wool." Is. 1:18 (NIV)

It seems to me quite odd
The name "Snow" was given to you by God.
God's design for snow is always cold
Yet your encouragement gently molds.

Snow waters, refreshing as it goes,
Quenching thirsty souls like the snow.
Your life style show you wait before the Father
For it is obvious, you seek no other.

Learning to become salt and light
Dear Jesus, make my heart white.
Whenever I get to make an angel in the snow
I'll thank God for the angel made in me by the Snows!

~ JC
2015

TODAY

Today when you ask for
your needs, ask, also, to
sit on His lap and to dwell
in His presence, to look
in His eyes.

As you behold His
Beauty, you find yourself
Becoming more like Him.
To bring true food to
The hungry souls you
Mix with every day.

To glimpse God with fresh eyes,
To bring hope on those dark days,
To be reminded how big God is,
To totally be embraced as His.
To walk hand in hand with Him,
To receive when resources are slim,
To know El Roi truly sees,
To understand, God brings all our needs.

~JC
2014

TOGETHER

It does my heart good to see father and family
Working together as they should

Building for God together a labor of love each one giving
The kids follow the father and mother

Who knows the price they give sacrificing and sharing
So others find Jesus and live

Strength and wisdom come their way because they study the
Word
And for the body, they faithfully pray

Children are in church because they copy their father if Jesus
works for dad,
they give the Lord a try

On your knees with heart lifted up, God makes a leader

Praying, and loving, mom is at your side She is cooking and
cleaning
Making a home of joy where the Spirit abides

I understand birthdays may not be your thing A smile and a
hug is good enough
My gift to you: Thanks - Your ministry makes my heart sing.

TRANSFORMED

Just as a door is opened and we can enter in
So must we open the door and let the Savior begin
He will open our eyes and remove our sin
His gentle touch and joy will happen.

He changes our heart. We are made anew.
Transforming the thoughts of me and you
Deep within I find life grew
Truly a miracle from God's hand I knew.

My eyes opened, Jesus I could see
Mercy and love He gave to me
Bringing freedom, truth, and liberty
God himself has set me free!

4-24-14

UNABLE TO ASK

Hot tears run down my face
I can't find peace any place
Maybe I'll drop out of the human race.

Deep inside a boiling pot dictates the day
It overflows into the angry words I say
Yet I can't stop the roar coming my way.

I do remember God's love for me
But to take His hand is impossibility
Fear and anger make me unruly.

Alone, no one knows how to care
I know I'm driven by confusion and fear
I just don't know how to get out of here.

Maybe someday I will see from the heavenlies
Why God chose this life for me
The scales will fall off and I shall behold His glory.

UNSEEN

Hope on the horizon
We tell ourselves each day.
Especially when it is dark
As we struggle along the way.

Can this be true?
Even when I look for it
My eyes are blinded and
My heart throws a fit.

Diligently, I look to the horizon
For hope to change me
Somehow I came up empty
Then I hear God speaking.

"My child, I am not over there"
"To receive hope, don't look so far."
"For I am walking right beside you"
"Unseen with your eyes but felt by your heart."

~JS
2019

UNLIKE TIME

Oh Lord, when will this broken heart end?
To have it to cease, I would like to pretend
Heal me so a new life can begin.

Why I still hurt I don't know
Every day I try to let go
Taking Your hand to help me grow.

Help me embrace what's most important to You
Bringing me that which can renew
Your presence heals, unlike time can do.

~JS

WATCHFUL EYE

Jesus wasn't even born at home
But what did it matter
For no place on earth was His home.

He came down from heaven
Left His Father who reigned on high
Knowing someday Jesus would return.

With a watchful eye
The Father watched Jesus,
Wandering from place to place,
Knowing the only home would be at His side,
In His true home in heaven, Jesus wanderings cease
Where there's love, joy and peace!

WORDS SPEAK

7-18-13

Someone handed me a life changing compliment. She said to me something I hadn't heard in a while. It dropped off my skills list a long time ago.

She said: "you're smart. Very often you answer your question even while presenting your need."

Bipolar Disorder has redirected my life, especially how I tell myself 'who I am'. I am always searching for evidence to prove that I am worthy and of value in my own eyes. I am empowered when my self-inspection declares that I have worth, and am worthy in the heart of someone else.

Bipolar may impair my body but it cannot steal my spirit.

WORKING GOD'S WAY

You? What can you do?
Even the simplest things are beyond you
Why do you even bother to try!
Hey! Just turn over and die!

"Expecting great works from your hands
"Ha!" In protest, others will just take a stand
With a steer, they wish you weren't even there
Hurt and angry, I try not to care.

The voice of God sweetly comes to me.
"My child, someday you will see"
"I made you how I wanted you to be
To grow lovingly with gifts of charity."

Working in God's hands
Makes your hands workable for God.

~JS
2018

YOU TWO

Of all the pastors I have ever had
I'm glad they were you.

Of all the churches I've attended
I'm glad I found yours.

Going through the Bible, verse by verse,
I'm glad you were teaching.

When passing out hugs,
I'm glad it was Janet and you.

With prayer to face life's challenges
I knew the two of you would be there.

When dark clouds seem to rule
You tow help me approach the Father.

When my flesh wants to reign
God equips you to bring me victory.

You two are a Heavenly Gift
God knows how much I need you.
~JS 2019

YUM-YUM

I was shopping for a creative, Halloween costume. My phone chimed. I pulled up the text. It said: "Bring me home a mummy."

Fortunately, we just hit the $ Store on the way home.

When I reached home, I was so proud having found this 6' bag of bones. With a smirk on my face, I opened the front door and handling over my cardboard treasure.

The joke was on me, see, the text was really: "Bring me a yummy!" "The request was general: Bring me anything sweet!"

Thinking there was a mistake, the phone text changed the "y" to a "m."

So often, we "help" God by making changings in His plans.

-JS
2017

CHRISTMAS

[[FOREIGN LANGUAGE]]

???lhnen kostenlos sprachliche Hilfsdienstleistungen
???: **711**).

???s d'aide linguistique vous sont proposés
???**11**).

Jesus is the Reason for the Season

JESUS IS BORN

Jesus is born? Jesus is born! The proclamation rings.
He is Lord of Lords and King of Kings.
Lying in a manger wrapped in swaddling clothes is He;
Wonderful, Counselor, the Mighty God;
who would destroy the enemy.

In a stable of a small Judean village He was born,
to break the yokes of bondage, and save the forlorn.
He now asks to be born within the hearts of mankind.
in Him can be found true joy and peace of mind.

The praises still go forth to Jesus Christ our King,
for He is Lord of Lords and Master of everything.
So join us and bring praises to His name
Blessed Redeemer, Beautiful Savior – He is evermore the same.

From your house to mine all across the miles,
Bringing Christmas closer, hope to make you smile.
Some say Santa is the reason why.
But I look to Jesus a bright star in the sky.
Bethlehem, the humble place of my Savior's birth
full of peace and joy, happiness and mirth.
He's coming again soon someday you'll see
To take us home for all eternity.
Are you ready? He's coming very soon.
It may be morning, night or noon.
So make this a day to remember. You gave your heart
to Jesus this December.
He washed your sins away making you white as snow.
Filling it with peace and happiness causing it to overflow.
This Christmas will be very special to you as you feel His joy,
purpose, and all brand new.
So take a moment and thank God for Jesus
for sending Him here to redeem us.
We praise Him for coming down from above,
Bringing hope and redemption – but most of all Love.
So when you think of Christmas this year,
Remember the Savior and all He brings dear
The manger and the cross go hand in hand
For they both bring hope all across the land.
MERRY CHRISTMAS

BECAUSE OF GOD'S WILL, HE CREATED MAN,
FROM THESE TWO THE WORLD BEGAN.
BECAUSE OF GOD'S NEED, HE LET THEM CHOOSE,
WHETHER TO WIN OR TO LOSE.
BECAUSE OF GOD'S GRACE, HE REPAIRED THE WAY,
HEALING TWO HEARTS GONE ASTRAY.
BECAUSE OF GOD'S LOVE, HE FORGOT THEIR DEED,
SINCE THEY ASKED HIM TO LEAD.

BECAUSE OF MAN'S WILL, HE PUT SELF ON THE THRONE,
HIS OWN LIFE TO RUN AND TO OWN.
BECAUSE OF MAN'S GREED, HE SOUGHT MORE GOODS
TO GAIN,
SEEKING PLEASURE NOT PAIN.
BECAUSE OF MAN'S PACE, HE LEFT HIS GOD FAR BEHIND,
SEARCHING FOR "GOLD" HE'D NEVER FIND.
BECAUSE OF MAN'S LOVE, HIS DEEPEST NEED HE'D
NEVER MEET,
FOR LOVE NEEDS GOD TO BE COMPLETE.

BECAUSE OF GOD'S WILL, HE GAVE HIS SON,
HIS VERY OWN BELOVED ONE.
BECAUSE OF GOD'S NEED, SIN'S DEBT MUST BE PAID,
SO ON HIS DEAR SON THIS LOAD HE LAID.
BECAUSE OF GOD'S GRACE, HE SET US FREE,
FROM SIN'S CURSE, IT'S RUIN AND TYRANNY.
BECAUSE OF GOD'S LOVE, HIS SON CAME DOWN,
SO THAT WE MIGHT TRADE THIS CROSS FOR HIS CROWN.

THE INVITATION

Then, God used the humble home of a stable,
where they house cows and sheep, to bring
His Son into the world.
    But, only after an invitation.

Today, God uses the humble home of our
hearts, where we house our fears and dreams,
To bring His Son to the world,
    But, only after an invitation.

Neither places are clean, only available.
Neither places are perfect, only freely given.
Neither places would we have chosen.
    But the, we are not God.

For God can bring: Honor to the humble,
    Strength to the suffering,
    Help to the hurting,
    Love to the lonely, and
    Answers to the asking.

All He needs is an invitation.

HAPPY BIRTHDAY!

For your birthday, Lord, what can I give you?
All I have you gave me because of your love so true.

How can I give you a gift you gave me?
That breaks the laws of kindness and courtesy

But, you know, Lord, it is the best I've got.
Only because of the grace you've brought.

Once I gave you my old life,
It was full of selfishness and strife

But I found a new life began to grow,
From within me, a love started to show.

So, for your birthday, I guess I'll give you me
Maybe you could use this gift to change eternity.

STARS

Looking up into the stars I see
A grand display of majesty!
Each star shines bright and clear
Makes me wonder why I'm here.
Like the stars, I too, shine in the night
with God's hope, bringing His light.

Long ago, God sent a star
to guide the wise men from afar.
Looking for the babe they hoped to find,
the One who would redeem mankind.
In with the animals, a manger was His bed,
just exactly as God Himself had said.

Why did God choose a barn this day,
for His heavenly Child to lay?
Among the horses, cows, and straw
Couldn't God choose better?...after all!
This was His Son, born as a man He came
His Salvation to the world proclaims!

~JC~
2012

MOTHER MARY

Espoused wife
Rejoicing hearts
Redeeming grace
YHWH in the flesh

Conceived by the Holy Spirit
Heavenly star
Righteousness personified
Immanuel
Son of God
Treasures given
Magi came
Adoration offered
Savior born

WHAT DO YOU THINK
OF ST. PADDY'S DAY?

A pot of gold, is it worth any price to pay?
Little Green Men? A Rainbow that caught glowing eyes?
As I put on my green, I heave a big sigh.
Could I be letting the important things slide by?
Laying down my green clover, I will give God a try.

I hear his love reaches farther than that bow in the sky
His mercy's worth more than money can buy
Yet He gives it free to you and I.
This may sound foolish but tis no lie
Talk to Jesus today, don't be shy
He'll bring purpose from chaos – this I can't deny!

J. C. 3-6-2013

Printed in the United States
By Bookmasters